Dear Parents,

Welcome to the Scholastic Reader series. We have taken over 80 years of experience with teachers, parents, and children and put it into a program that is designed to match your child's interests and skills.

Level 1—Short sentences and stories made up of words kids can sound out using their phonics skills and words that are important to remember.

Level 2—Longer sentences and stories with words kids need to know and new "big" words that they will want to know.

Level 3—From sentences to paragraphs to longer stories, these books have large "chunks" of texts and are made up of a rich vocabulary.

Level 4—First chapter books with more words and fewer pictures.

It is important that children learn to read well enough to succeed in school and beyond. Here are ideas for reading this book with your child:

• Look at the book together. Encourage your child to read the title and make a prediction about the story.
• Read the book together. Encourage your child to sound out words when appropriate. When your child struggles, you can help by providing the word.
• Encourage your child to retell the story. This is a great way to check for comprehension.
• Have your child take the fluency test on the last page to check progress.

Scholastic Readers are designed to support your child's efforts to learn how to read at every age and every stage. Enjoy helping your child learn to read and love to read.

—Francie Alexander
Chief Education Officer
Scholastic Education

For Brian, pumpkin pie baker extraordinaire
—J.E.G.

For my grandfather (Pap)
who first showed me the joys of gardening.
—T.S-L.

Text copyright © 2000 by Jane E. Gerver.
Illustrations copyright © 2000 by Tammie Speer-Lyon.
Fluency activities copyright © 2003 Scholastic Inc.

All rights reserved. Published by Scholastic Inc.
SCHOLASTIC, CARTWHEEL BOOKS, and associated logos are trademarks
and/or registered trademarks of Scholastic Inc.

Library of Congress Cataloging-in-Publication Data is available.

ISBN 0-439-59733-1

10 9 8 7 6 5

Printed in the U.S.A.   23
First printing, September 2000

GROW A PUMPKIN PIE!

by **Jane E. Gerver**

Illustrated by **Tammie Speer-Lyon**

Scholastic Reader — Level 1

SCHOLASTIC INC.

New York   Toronto   London   Auckland   Sydney
Mexico City   New Delhi   Hong Kong   Buenos Aires

Dig a hole.

Plant a seed.

Water well.

Pull a weed.

Here comes rain.

Splash in mud!

Shoots come up.

Then a bud.

Look! We see

a long green vine.

Little pumpkins grow

in a line.

The air gets cold.

Leaves fall down—

orange, yellow,

red, and brown.

Pumpkins ripen

on the ground.

Pick one that is
big and round.

Cut the top.

Start to scoop.

Add eggs and cream.

It looks like soup.

Stir in sugar

with your spoon.

Hurry, hurry!

It's almost noon!

Mix in spices.

Let's be quick!

Stir some more.

Now it's thick.

Pour it in

a crusty shell.

Place in the oven.

Bake it well.

It must cool.

Let it sit.

Take a fork.

Taste a bit.

Don't forget

to save a seed.

Plant it next year—

it's all you need!

What Comes First?

What comes first? What comes second?
What comes third? What comes last?

Match the Pumpkins

Which pumpkins are small? Which ones are
tall? Which ones are round? Which ones are
lumpy and bumpy?

Pumpkin Patch Maze

Find the way through the maze. Start at the gate.
End at the pumpkin patch. Don't cross any lines
along the way!

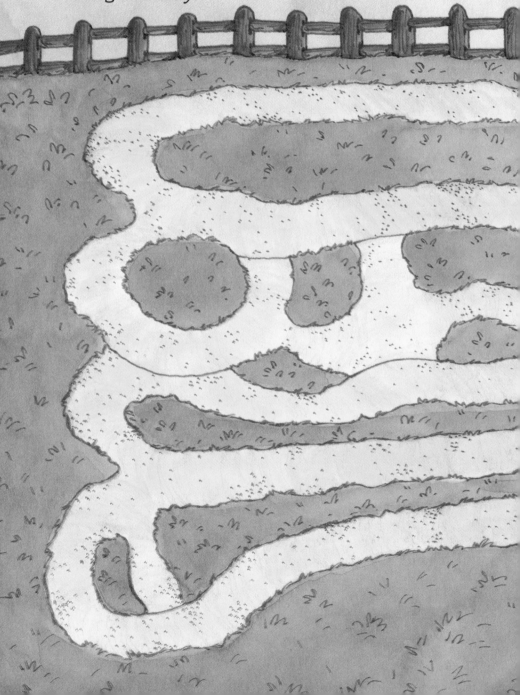

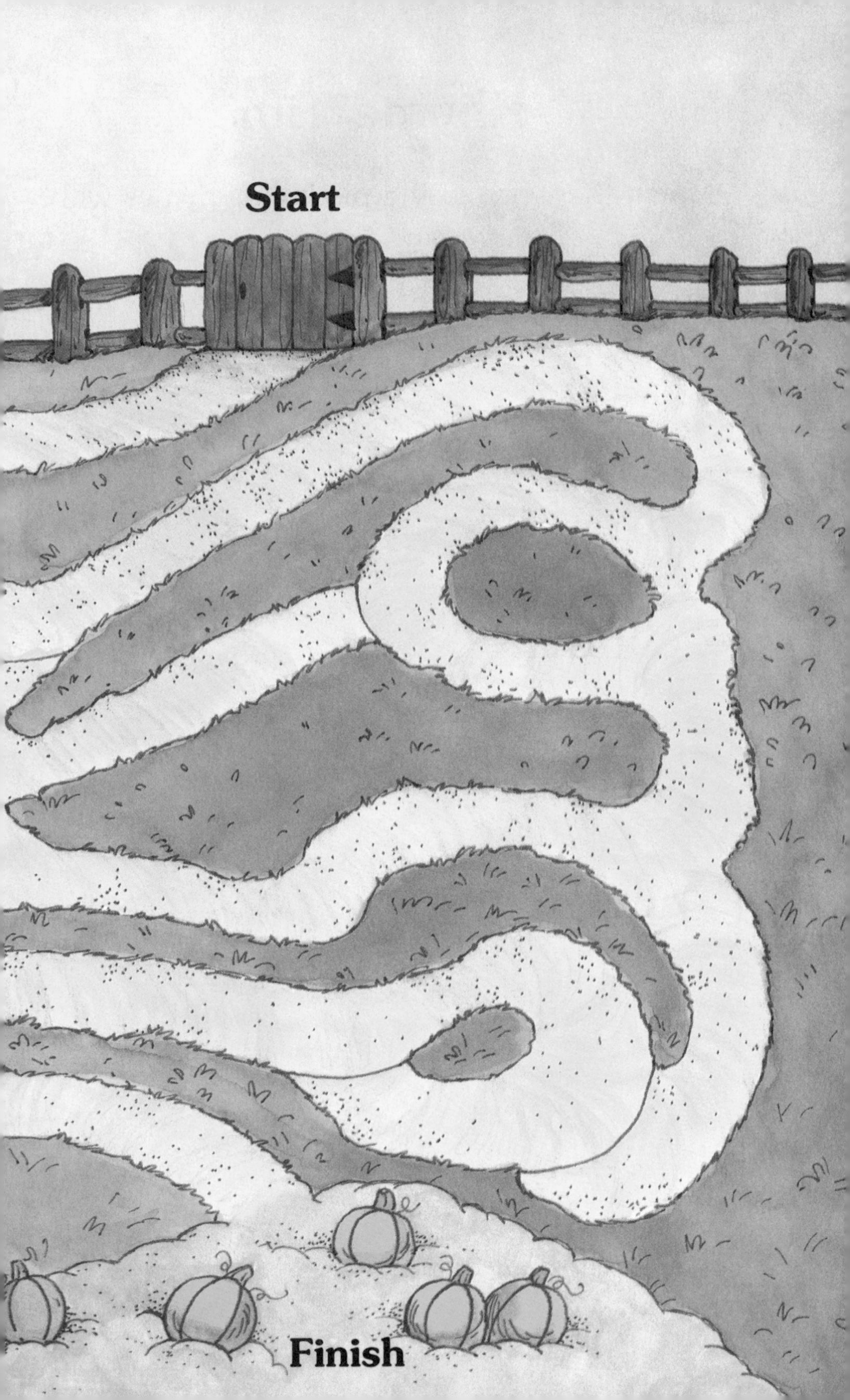
Start
Finish

Rhyme Time

Match the word to the picture it rhymes with.

dig

line

noon

weed

Pumpkin Faces

Draw a face on this pumpkin with a crayon
or a pencil. Is your pumpkin happy or sad?
Is your pumpkin awake or sleepy?

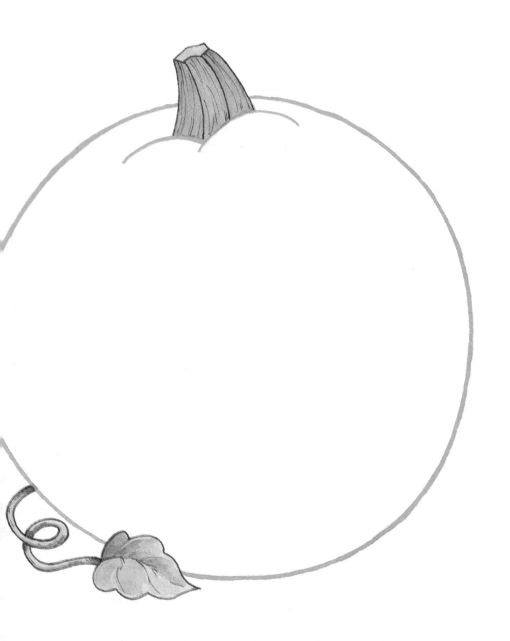

ANSWERS

What Comes First?

first   second   third   fourth

Pumpkin Patch Maze

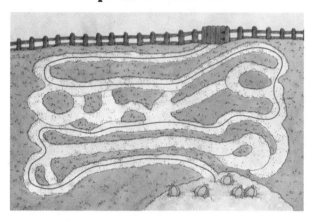

Match the Pumpkins

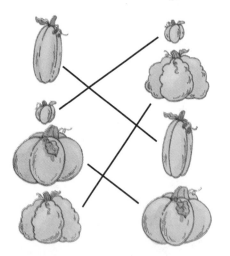

Rhyme Time

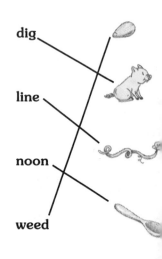

dig

line

noon

weed